ALICE LIVEING

Unveiling the Warrior Within:

Alice Liveing's Journey from

Turmoil to Triumph

Table of Contents

Foreword 5

Introduction 11

Chapter One 19

   The Turning Point 19

Chapter Two 32

   Shadows and Strength 32

Chapter Three 46

   Escaping the Darkness 46

Chapter Four 59

   Reclaiming Control 59

Chapter Five 74

   Evolution and Empowerment 74

Chapter Six 89

   Balancing Act 89

Chapter Seven 105

Healing and Hope 105

Chapter Eight..................................119

Give Me Strength........................119

Foreword

In a world where social media often presents an idealized version of life, it is uncommon to find someone who is brave enough to reveal their true, unfiltered self. Alice Liveing is one of those rare individuals.

In this captivating biography, we are taken on a journey through the ups and downs of

Alice's life—a journey that is both inspiring and heartbreaking. From the outside, Alice seemed to have it all: a successful career as a personal trainer, a large following on Instagram, and bestselling books. However, beneath the surface, there was a darkness that threatened to consume her.

As we delve into Alice's story, we uncover the painful truth of her past—a past filled with abuse, trauma, and self-destructive behavior. From her early struggles with weight and body image to a toxic relationship that almost destroyed her, Alice's journey showcases the resilience of the human spirit.

But this is not just a tale of suffering; it is also a story of redemption and triumph. Through sheer determination and unwavering bravery, Alice found the strength to confront her demons head-on. She sought help, faced her fears, and emerged stronger and more resilient than ever before.

In these pages, you will witness the incredible transformation of a woman who refused to let her past define her. She found her voice, regained her power, and became an inspiration to others. Alice shares her story with honesty, vulnerability, and a touch of humor, inviting us to join her on a journey of self-discovery and healing.

Get ready to be captivated, because Alice Liveing's story is a thrilling rollercoaster of emotions, intrigue, and ultimately, triumph. As you read through this biography, you will be reminded that no matter how difficult things may seem, there is always hope on the horizon. Sometimes, the greatest strength comes from embracing the darkness and emerging into the light.

Introduction

In a society where social media often presents an idealized version of people's lives, Alice Liveing's story serves as a beacon of truth, reminding us that behind every carefully curated image lies a complex and often untold story. Through her posts, captions, and thoughtfully crafted images,

Alice invites her followers into a world that is both raw and genuine, while also inspiring.

However, the path to authenticity was not an easy one for Alice. Growing up in the charming town of Gerrards Cross, England, her childhood was filled with both happiness and sadness. From a young age, she struggled with her weight, feeling like an outsider in a society that prioritized thinness above all else. But it wasn't just societal pressures that burdened Alice; she also carried the weight of her mother's own struggles with weight and self-image.

As Alice navigated the challenging waters of adolescence, she found solace in the world of dance. Each graceful movement provided her with a sense of freedom and self-expression that couldn't be found elsewhere. However, even as she pursued her passion for dance, Alice couldn't escape the harsh reality of the world around her. She faced bullying at school and battled with self-doubt, yearning for acceptance and a sense of belonging.

Alice reached a turning point in her life in her early twenties, which would have a profound impact on her future. After graduating from Bird College of

Performing Arts, she embarked on a journey of self-discovery, where she confronted the personal struggles that had haunted her for a long time.

By creating her Instagram account, Clean Eating Alice, she began documenting her pursuit of health and fitness. This journey was not only about physical transformation but also about self-acceptance. Through her posts, she shared both her successes and setbacks, inspiring others to embark on their own path towards well-being.

However, Alice faced numerous challenges on her path to success. Behind the polished image of social media, she dealt with personal hardships that she had encountered throughout her life. From an abusive relationship to online trolls, she experienced adversity. Nevertheless, she remained true to herself and used her platform to shed light on the less glamorous aspects of human existence.

This biography takes a deep dive into the life of Alice Liveing, showcasing her resilience, courage, and authenticity. It explores her journey from humble beginnings in Gerrards Cross to becoming a social media sensation. Alice's story is one of overcoming challenges, finding hope in difficult times, and maintaining unwavering belief that the dawn will always come after the darkest night. Join us on this captivating and inspiring journey through the ups and downs of Alice's life, filled with suspense and heartwarming moments. Through this biography, you will discover the extraordinary tale of a woman who defied the odds, embraced her truth, and emerged stronger and more resilient than ever before.

Chapter One
The Turning Point

In Gerrards Cross, the morning sun shone through the thick trees that lined the suburban streets, creating patterns of light on the pavement. Nine-year-old Alice Liveing hurried to her primary school, feeling burdened by the memories of the previous night. The cruel words of a stranger towards her mother still echoed in her mind: "Move out of the way, you fat b****." Despite her mother's efforts to shield her children from such ugliness, Alice could see the pain in her eyes. As they walked home in silence, Alice couldn't forget the image of her defeated mother and her own helplessness in protecting her.

Life in Gerrards Cross was a mix of beautiful landscapes and the unspoken pressures of societal expectations. The Liveing family home was filled with love and support, but underneath it all was a constant struggle - her mother's battle with weight, a problem that seemed to affect every aspect of their lives.

Alice's mother was not just large in size, but she was

deeply unhappy with her appearance. It went beyond just wanting to look good or fit societal standards; it was about her ability to move, her health, and her longing for a life free from physical limitations. Alice could see this in the way her mother would gaze longingly at the trampoline in their backyard, where she and her siblings would bounce around with boundless energy, a place her mother could never join. Every meal became a battle between wanting to eat healthily and feeling guilty for indulging, with each bite carrying the weight of wanting to be thinner rather than being nourished.

Alice learned early on about resilience. She was bullied at school for reasons she couldn't understand, but she found comfort in her mother's wise words: "Bullying is a reflection of the bully, not the victim. It's their problem, not yours." This mantra, repeated with love and firmness, became a shield against the daily insults and hurtful words. However, even with this armor of resilience, each taunt still left its mark.

As Alice got older, she constantly carried the memory of her mother's struggle, which influenced her views on food, body image, and self-value. She witnessed her mother trying numerous diets that promised success but only resulted in disappointment. The focus was always on losing weight, never on gaining health or happiness. Exercise was seen as a form of punishment rather than a celebration of the body's capabilities. This cycle of hope and despair became a familiar pattern in their home.

However, everything changed for Alice in her early twenties, a time when most of her peers were enjoying the freedoms and indulgences of young adulthood. For Alice, it was a moment of realization. Years of observing her mother's battle, combined with her own experiences of bullying and self-doubt, led to a strong determination. She refused to let others' opinions or her own insecurities define her. Instead, she decided to take control of her own story, transforming both her body and mind in the process.

After graduating from Bird College of performing arts, Alice had a decision to make: pursue a career in the arts or follow a path that had been quietly calling her for years. She chose the latter and fully immersed herself in the world of fitness. Her goal was not only to transform her own life but also to inspire and educate others. Alice started her Instagram account, Clean Eating Alice, where she documented her journey from unhealthy eating habits to a balanced and vibrant lifestyle.

Her followers quickly multiplied, drawn to her authenticity and the relatable struggle of a young woman striving for self-improvement. Through her posts, which featured tempting dishes and invigorating workout routines, Alice offered a glimpse into a life of balance and wellness.

However, beneath the surface, a deeper mission was taking shape. Alice wanted to use her platform for a greater purpose, particularly to support women who, like her mother and herself, had faced societal expectations and personal challenges.

Alice's story became more than just about fitness; it became about empowerment. She was prepared to face the world not only as a personal trainer and influencer but also as an advocate for women's health and well-being. This journey had only just begun, and as she stood on the threshold of this new chapter, the lessons from her past experiences - the pain, the resilience, and the unwavering support of her family - fueled her determination to make a meaningful impact.

This is the narrative of Alice Liveing, a story of change and success, of converting suffering into a meaningful mission. It starts with a young girl in Gerrards Cross attending a concert, but it extends much further, impacting the lives of countless individuals she motivates on a daily basis.

Chapter Two
Shadows and Strength

The first sign of trouble emerged subtly and harmlessly. Alice Liveing, a sixteen-year-old girl filled with excitement from her first romantic relationship, was swept off her feet by Charles. He showed attentiveness in ways that made her feel flattered, as a young girl yearning for affection and validation. He constantly texted her, eager to know every detail of her life. Initially, it felt like a warm and secure embrace. However, as time passed, this embrace became constricting and suffocating.

Charles's attentiveness was not the caring concern that Alice initially believed it to be. It was control disguised as care. His constant questioning about her whereabouts, his jealousy towards any interaction with other boys, and his demands to see her phone were all early warning signs that Alice, in her innocence, mistook for deep affection. She repeatedly told herself, "He just really cares about me," even as doubts started to creep into her mind.

The illusion shattered on a scorching summer day. Alice had gone to watch Charles play football, a regular weekend activity that was meant to bring joy. The sun was high, the sky was a vibrant blue, and Alice was wearing her favorite shorts, enjoying the warmth on her skin. As they drove back, an unspoken tension seemed to fill the air in the car. A thoughtless comment—she couldn't even recall what she had said—

triggered him. In an instant, his hand struck her leg with such force that it left her stunned.

Alice vividly remembers the moment she burst into tears and expressed her disbelief and shock at being hit by Charles. The pain she felt went beyond physical; it was a deep betrayal from someone who claimed to care for her. Charles responded coldly and dismissively, downplaying the significance of his actions. However, for Alice, it was a pivotal moment that revealed the true nature of their relationship.

Despite the initial shock and hurt, Alice found herself caught in a cycle of confusion and denial. She desperately wanted to believe that this incident was a one-time mistake, not recognizing it as domestic abuse at the time. The subsequent apologies, promises, and temporary return to the attentive boyfriend she thought she knew blurred the reality of her situation.

Unfortunately, the violence didn't end there. It only escalated, intertwining with emotional manipulation. Charles isolated Alice from her friends and made her feel guilty for seeking support or comfort outside of their relationship.

His words were more damaging than any physical blow, constantly belittling her, undermining her self-confidence, and causing her to question her own worth. Despite her youth, Alice struggled to reconcile the love she felt with the fear that now tainted every interaction.

It took Alice many years to fully understand the extent of the abuse she had endured. It took even longer for her to break free from it. Instead of a dramatic escape, she gradually took small but determined steps towards reclaiming her life. Throughout this difficult journey, she relied on her family for unwavering support, which helped her navigate the challenging process of healing. Although there were setbacks and moments of despair, she also made profound discoveries about her own strength and resilience.

It wasn't until more than eight years after the initial incident that Alice found the courage to share her experiences. By that time, she had transformed her life in various ways, becoming a role model for health and fitness and inspiring others through her presence on social media and work as a personal trainer. However, the memories of her past still haunted her, serving as a reminder of the battles she had fought and the inner strength she had discovered.

In a powerful move to reclaim her own story, Alice announced that she had become a celebrity ambassador for Women's Aid. Standing before a room full of supporters, she spoke openly about the abuse she had endured, her voice steady and strong. This moment was not only liberating for her, but also for many others who saw their own struggles reflected in her story.

"I believed he genuinely cared about me," she expressed, her gaze scanning the crowd. "However, I have come to realize that true care does not involve control, harm, or belittlement. I am here to assert that nobody should be subjected to such treatment. And if sharing my story can empower even one person to recognize their worth and gather the courage to leave, then it is worthwhile."

As Alice stood there, the applause surrounding her, she experienced a profound sense of closure. The dark remnants of her past no longer had power over her. She confronted them, uttered their names, and in doing so, took the initial steps towards not just surviving, but thriving. This phase of her life, once defined by pain, had now become a testament to her resilience and unwavering dedication to assisting others in finding their strength.

Alice Liveing's journey was far from complete. She had transformed her pain into a sense of purpose, and each day she continued to inspire, educate, and advocate. The girl who once felt trapped in the shadows had emerged into the light, prepared to illuminate the path for others to follow.

Chapter Three
Escaping the Darkness

Alice sat in the passenger seat of Charles's car, reminiscing about her carefree childhood days as the scorching summer sun beat down on her. She couldn't help but wonder how her life had taken such a dark turn. Suddenly, she was brought back to reality by a sharp, unexpected pain as Charles slapped her leg with force, causing a burning sensation to spread. Tears streamed down her face as she confronted him, but his response was swift and cruel, a pattern she would unfortunately become all too familiar with.

In disbelief and filled with shock and betrayal, Alice sobbed, questioning Charles, "I can't believe you just hit me. What on earth, Charles?"

Charles immediately and persistently apologized, showering her with gifts, taking her out to fancy dinners, and overwhelming her with affection. In that moment, it felt as if the violent incident had never occurred. However, this relief was always short-lived. The cycle would repeat itself: an outburst of anger followed by an excessive display of kindness that left Alice trapped in a whirlwind of confusion and self-blame.

"He would make me believe it was my fault," Alice later reflected. "He would say that I provoked him to the point where he had no other choice but to hit me. Eventually, I started to believe him."

Charles had a strong hold over Alice that went beyond their physical encounters. He made sure that Alice was cut off from her friends and family, constantly demanding to know where she was. Even innocent outings with friends turned into intense questioning sessions.

Alice's social life completely disappeared as her entire world revolved around Charles's desires and emotions.

Alice admitted, "I stopped going out with friends and attending family gatherings. I didn't want my parents to find out about the situation. If I was even briefly out of Charles's sight, he would accuse me of being unfaithful."

The feeling of being alone and cut off from others was overwhelming. Alice's loved ones noticed her withdrawal, but she was too scared to seek help. She felt trapped in every sense, both physically and emotionally. The burden of her secret was crushing, but she was even more afraid of the consequences that would come with revealing the truth.

The abuse continued to escalate. What started as slaps and bites turned into sexual assaults. Charles's anger seemed limitless. During a heated argument one night, he bit into the back of her arm with such force that the bite marks remained visible for weeks. When a friend at school asked about the marks in the locker room, Alice lied and said she had accidentally closed her arm in a car door.

"I felt completely trapped," she explained. "I couldn't confide in anyone. I was terrified of him."

Alice's attempts to break free were met with threats and manipulation. On one occasion, Charles sat on the edge of a railway bridge, crying and threatening to jump if she left him. Distraught and overwhelmed at the age of sixteen, Alice could do nothing but cry uncontrollably.

Alice finally mustered the courage to end the relationship after enduring a terrifying and distressing eighteen months. However, Charles refused to accept the breakup and persistently called her house at all hours, causing disturbance to her family. To find some solace, they had to disconnect the phone.

Alice vividly remembers her fear of Charles showing up at her doorstep and the anxiety of going outside. Unfortunately, her fears became a reality when, a few days after their split, Charles unexpectedly appeared while she was walking between school campuses. He recklessly drove his car onto the pavement, accompanied by a friend and wielding a baseball bat. He forcefully pushed Alice against a wall and subjected her to a brutal assault. This horrifying incident was witnessed by several bystanders and captured on security cameras.

The police swiftly intervened, resulting in Charles being charged with causing physical harm. The court issued a restraining order and sentenced him to community service. This marked the last time Alice saw him, but the scars he left extended far beyond the surface.

While the physical abuse was undeniably terrible, the emotional trauma endured by Alice lasted much longer. She acknowledged that it is not a matter of one being worse than the other, but the emotional abuse was significantly more challenging to recover from.

After Charles left her, Alice initiated the extensive process of recovery. Although she managed to endure the ordeal, merely surviving was merely the initial phase. At this point, she had to regain control of her life, reconstruct her self-assurance, and rediscover the ability to place faith in others. This expedition would span several years, but Alice was resolute in her determination to embark on this journey.

Chapter Four

Reclaiming Control

Alice's breakup with Charles was not just a separation from a person; it was a separation from a past filled with fear and manipulation. However, the emotional scars from those eighteen months did not disappear after the court verdict. They remained deeply ingrained in her mind, affecting her life in various ways. One of the most significant effects was her relationship with food.

For a long time, Alice found comfort in overeating as a way to cope with her unresolved emotions. Food provided a temporary escape from the pain and gave her a fleeting sense of control in a world that had been dominated by Charles's unpredictable cruelty. However, this comfort was deceptive, leading to a cycle of guilt and self-hatred that further damaged her self-confidence.

In an interview with *Cosmopolitan UK*, Alice reflected, "When you come out of an abusive relationship, you really have to start from scratch and rebuild yourself. It's not easy, but I discovered that regaining control over something that had spiraled out of my control was my way of doing it."

The turning point occurred on a cold winter morning when Alice, burdened by her past, stood in front of the mirror. She not only noticed the physical changes but also the emotional baggage she had accumulated. A strong determination surged within her, and she decided that her story would not end this way. Taking control back, she started with her diet, the one thing she could manage.

And so, Clean Eating Alice was born. It started as a personal journey, a commitment to embrace a healthier lifestyle. She began by making small changes, replacing processed foods with fresh produce and sugary snacks with wholesome alternatives. The progress was slow but each step forward felt like reclaiming her independence. Preparing nutritious meals became a healing ritual, a way to nourish her body and spirit.

Alice shared her journey on Instagram, not seeking followers but to hold herself accountable. However, her authenticity, vulnerability, and unwavering determination resonated with many. Her follower count started growing, forming a community of people inspired by her transformation. Clean Eating Alice evolved from just an Instagram account into a movement.

Her journey was not just focused on losing weight, but also on overcoming the emotional pain and rebuilding herself from within. Each healthy meal and workout made Alice feel stronger and more in control. The online community she created offered support and encouragement, helping her stay on track even when she was tempted to fall back into old habits.

However, Alice's mission went beyond her own personal transformation. She wanted to give back and use her platform to help others who were going through the same struggles she had faced. Becoming an ambassador for Women's Aid was a natural step towards achieving this goal. She hoped to spread a message that she herself had desperately needed to hear when she was 16.

"I wish I had something that made me realize I wasn't alone. That what I was going through was real and deserving of help," she said, her voice reflecting the weight of her experiences.

As an ambassador for Women's Aid, Alice shared her story to shed light on the hidden nature of domestic abuse, how it distorts one's perception of reality, and erodes self-worth. She openly discussed the emotional manipulation, physical violence, and the long journey to recovery. Her honesty helped break the silence surrounding such abuse and offered hope to others in similar situations.

The impact was significant. Women who had found the courage to leave abusive relationships reached out, inspired by Alice's story. Others shared their ongoing struggles, grateful to know they were not alone. Each message served as a reminder of the importance of her work, motivating her to stay committed to the cause.

Alice's partnership with Women's Aid went beyond raising awareness; it involved advocating and taking action. She participated in campaigns, spoke at events, and worked tirelessly to ensure that resources were accessible for those in need. Her goal was to create a world where no one felt trapped or helpless, where everyone understood their value and had the support to rebuild their lives.

The journey from being a victim to becoming a survivor, from a girl controlled by fear to a woman empowered by her own strength, was long and filled with challenges. However, Alice Liveing emerged from her past not only as a survivor but also as a symbol of hope and resilience. Clean Eating Alice represented more than just a personal brand; it demonstrated the power of taking control, transforming pain into purpose, and using one's platform to make a positive impact.

Alice's narrative, previously entrenched in the depths of mistreatment, had undergone a remarkable change, embodying a tale of personal growth, empowerment, and unwavering optimism. Starting from scratch, she had managed to rebuild herself, and in the process, she had illuminated a route for others to emulate. The remnants of her past no longer dictated her identity; instead, they emphasized the fortitude and tenacity that now emanated from her, serving as a source of inspiration for numerous individuals to discover their own journey towards liberation and recovery.

Chapter Five
Evolution and Empowerment

Alice Liveing's social media presence showcased her vibrant personality, which was the result of significant physical and emotional transformations over the years. Through her posts, Alice not only inspired her followers with her commitment to fitness, health, and overall well-being but also provided glimpses into her personal journey. However, beneath the carefully curated images and motivational captions, there was a much deeper, intricate, and intensely personal story.

After amassing a dedicated following on Instagram over a span of four years, Alice felt a new sense of purpose. While social media had allowed her to connect with thousands of people through concise posts, she yearned for a platform that would enable her to delve deeper, share more, and establish a more profound connection. This longing ultimately led her to create her own personal website, where she could share longer and more comprehensive content.

Alice declared in her first blog post that she has a lot she wants to write about, including topics such as fitness, fashion, skincare, lifestyle, and more. She encourages her readers to engage with her and suggest future topics for her to write about. Her website is a valuable resource for her followers, providing insights into her daily routines, favorite recipes, and tips for maintaining a balanced lifestyle. However, beneath the surface of these posts lies the powerful reason why Alice has become so dedicated to health and wellness. Her remarkable transformation and lifestyle change were not solely driven by a desire to look good or conform to societal standards. They were a result of a much deeper need – to regain control, heal, and rebuild herself after the trauma she experienced in her youth. The same trauma that once led her to seek solace in unhealthy eating habits has now propelled her towards a path of holistic wellness.

After leaving Charles, Alice experienced a time of profound self-exploration. She was resolute in not allowing the abuse she endured to define her, but instead, she wanted to be known for how she overcame it. Fitness became her refuge, and the gym became a haven where she could concentrate on developing her physical and mental strength. Every time she lifted weights or ran a mile, she felt herself becoming more robust and resilient. The endorphins released during her workouts aided in dispelling the lasting effects of her past, filling her with a feeling of empowerment.

Alice's transformation from being a victim to becoming a victor was not a quick or easy process. She encountered numerous obstacles, moments of self-doubt, and reminders of her past relationship. However, with the support of her family, friends, and an ever-growing online community, she persevered. She used her pain to fuel her purpose, turning her Instagram account into Clean Eating Alice, which became a source of inspiration for many.

What made Alice's posts resonate with her followers was not just their visual appeal, but also the genuine and authentic nature behind them. She openly shared her struggles, successes, and ongoing journey of self-improvement. This transparency created a sense of trust and connection with her audience, many of whom found comfort and motivation in her words.

However, Alice wanted to do more than just inspire through pictures and brief captions. She wanted to share her entire story, offering a narrative that could serve as a lifeline for those facing similar challenges. Her website became a platform for this extended storytelling, allowing her to delve deeper into topics and provide her followers with practical advice and insights.

Alice shared the distressing details of her abusive relationship and her journey to rebuild her life in one of her initial lengthy posts. She discussed the nights she spent crying, the days of feeling completely lost, and the small steps she took towards healing. Her words were honest, unfiltered, and deeply touching.

In her post, Alice mentioned that, like many fitness influencers, she went through a significant physical transformation and a change in lifestyle. However, there was more to her story than what initially meets the eye. She had a compelling reason for prioritizing her health and well-being.

Alice's story was not just about survival; it was also about resilience and empowerment. It demonstrated the human spirit's ability to overcome adversity and turn pain into a driving force. Her followers, who now read her blog, saw their own struggles reflected in her story and found hope that they too could find a way out of their own darkness.

The website quickly gained popularity, with eager readers eagerly anticipating each new post. They left comments, sharing their own experiences and expressing gratitude to Alice for her honesty. The community she had built on Instagram now had a new platform where they could engage more deeply and find even greater support.

Alice's journey was far from over. As she continued to grow and change, she remained dedicated to her mission of inspiring others to take control of their health and well-being. Her platform, which had become more diverse, allowed her to reach even more people, share more of her knowledge, and have an even greater impact.

The girl who had once felt completely trapped had found her freedom, and in doing so, had become a guiding light for others. Through fitness, health, and the power of her own story, Alice Liveing had not only transformed her own life but had also touched the lives of countless others, proving that it is possible to overcome the darkest times and emerge stronger, more empowered, and ready to conquer the world.

Chapter Six
Balancing Act

Alice Liveing's journey to success in the fitness industry was not a straightforward path, but rather a story of resilience, dedication, and the unwavering support of her family. Before she became known as Clean Eating Alice and gained a large following on Instagram, Alice's first passion was performing on stage.

She started her career as a professional dancer and performer, traveling around the UK with a musical. The demanding schedule and the challenges of life as a performer taught her discipline, which later became a fundamental aspect of her fitness philosophy. However, when her time in the spotlight came to an end, Alice found herself at a crossroads. Transitioning from a performer to a personal trainer was not easy, but she made the decision based on her own transformative journey towards health and fitness.

"Becoming a personal trainer felt like the natural next step," Alice said. "I had personally experienced a significant lifestyle change and developed a genuine passion for strength and conditioning. The physical and mental benefits it brought me were life-changing, and I wanted to share that with others."

Alice became a certified personal trainer four years ago and dedicated herself to her new career with the same passion she had once reserved for performing on stage. She initially worked at a well-known gym in London and later moved to Third Space Soho, where she started working with clients individually. Alice's commitment to continuous learning allowed her to stay up-to-date with the latest fitness trends and provide excellent service to her clients.

In addition to her personal training work, Alice also ventured into writing. From 2016 to 2017, she published books that shared her personal journey and insights, connecting with a wider audience through her clear and relatable writing style. This further established her as a prominent figure in the fitness industry. Her success led to a regular column in *Women's Health* magazine, where she discussed the latest trends and offered expert advice to readers.

Alice's accomplishments extended beyond the gym and

writing. She collaborated with Primark to release two highly popular activewear collections, one of which received the prestigious Draper's award for best influencer collaboration. These milestones showcased her ability to inspire others through various mediums.

Alice's professional life flourished, but her personal life was greatly influenced by her mother's transformation. Over the past ten years, Alice's mother had worked hard to change her mindset and behavior, becoming more grounded and calm. Alice acknowledged that while her job involved helping strangers change their lifestyles, her mother had accomplished it all on her own, which she found impressive. She believed it was important to maintain a certain level of separation between her work and family life, as she didn't want to constantly analyze her mother's choices at home.

This balance between professional success and personal boundaries was crucial for Alice. Despite her high profile, she remained down-to-earth and credited her mother's support for helping her navigate the pressures of her career. Whenever she faced online bullying, her mother would send her a message asking if she was okay, which meant a lot to Alice.

Alice admitted that online bullying was a sad reality of being an influencer. However, she had learned to be resilient, and knowing that her mother was on her side helped her cope with it.

Becoming an influencer was not an easy journey for Alice. She was open about her struggles with online criticism and shared honest reflections on her path, which resonated with her followers. This authenticity, combined with her expertise, made her a trusted figure in the fitness community.

Alice's impact went beyond her Instagram account and professional accomplishments. She also took photos with TV personalities like Melanie Sykes, which expanded her reach and visibility. However, despite the glamour and recognition, Alice stayed focused on her main goal: to inspire and empower others through fitness and wellness.

As Alice evolved, so did her platforms. Her website became a central place for longer posts, allowing her to share more detailed content about fitness, fashion, skincare, lifestyle, and more. She announced that she had many topics she wanted to write about and encouraged her audience to provide feedback and suggest future posts or articles.

Her story was one of transformation, not just physically but in all aspects of her life. Alice had built her career based on her personal experiences, using her past challenges to inform her work and motivate her followers.

Every post, client session, and collaboration was a step forward in her journey of self-improvement and empowerment.

As her influence grew, Alice remained dedicated to using her platform for positive purposes. She continued to advocate for mental health, drawing from her own experiences to offer support and encouragement to those in need. Her role as a celebrity ambassador for Women's Aid demonstrated her commitment to helping others overcome their struggles and find their inner strength.

Alice Liveing's narrative was not yet complete. Every phase of her life contributed to her character, making her the inspirational figure she is today. Her experiences, no matter how difficult, served as a reminder that they can ultimately lead to remarkable personal development and change. As Alice anticipated what lay ahead, she was prepared to keep motivating others, one social media post, one workout session, and one personal story at a time.

Chapter Seven
Healing and Hope

Alice Liveing had always faced challenges with resilience, but her journey to finding love again was particularly difficult. Her previous relationship with Charles had left her emotionally scarred and struggling with trust issues.

The thought of opening her heart again seemed almost impossible, but fate had other plans.

In 2016, Alice came across Patrick on a dating app. Patrick, a calm and kind 32-year-old, stood out from anyone she had ever known. Their initial conversations were cautious, each message a small step towards building trust. However, Patrick's patience and genuine care slowly broke down the walls Alice had built around her heart.

"Meeting Patrick was like a breath of fresh air," Alice reminisced. "With him, I could let my guard down and be my true self. He loved me for who I was, and that feeling was incredible."

Living together strengthened their connection. Patrick's

unwavering support provided Alice with a safe haven where she could continue to heal and grow. Their relationship was a complete contrast to the turmoil she had experienced with Charles. Instead of fear and manipulation, there was trust and mutual respect.

However, life had its difficulties. Two years ago, Alice received a diagnosis of polycystic ovary syndrome

(PCOS), a condition that could potentially impact her ability to conceive. While this news was devastating, Alice remained hopeful. She had aspirations of starting a family and was determined not to let her condition dictate her future.

"When that time comes," Alice expressed, "I want to adopt my mother's hands-off approach to parenting. She allowed me to learn from my own mistakes and find my own path, while always being there to support me when I needed it. That's the kind of mother I aspire to be."

Sarah Liveing, who is now 59 years old, resided in Buckinghamshire with her husband of three decades, Chris. Observing Alice navigate her public life brought both pride and concern to Sarah. Alice had always possessed a captivating personality. From a young age, people were drawn to her friendly nature and fearless spirit. Sarah recognized that her daughter's charm would open doors for her, but she also understood the negative aspects of being in the public eye.

"It's not always easy having a daughter in the public eye," Sarah confessed. "The tragic death of Caroline Flack has shown us the very real consequences of the online abuse that people like Alice endure on a daily basis."

Sarah and Alice had regular conversations and maintained a strong bond. However, Sarah also kept up with Alice's life through Instagram, where she would see her daughter's daily activities and read the comments from followers. While the positive feedback was uplifting, the negative comments were difficult for Sarah to handle.

Sarah mentioned that, like Alice, she would never engage with the trolls. She had to trust in Alice's strength and hope that if she needed support, she would reach out. Sarah felt incredibly proud of Alice for her honesty. Alice was a refreshing contrast to the culture of perfection on social media, as she openly shared her struggles and aimed to present a normal image, even if it went against the mainstream.

Alice's openness about her life, including her past abuse and ongoing battles with PCOS, deeply resonated with her followers. Her refusal to pretend to be perfect made her relatable and beloved. She demonstrated that strength could come from vulnerability and that it was possible to overcome adversity while still maintaining hope for the future.

At one point, the legacy of abuse had threatened to overshadow Alice's life, but she had taken back control of her story. Her relationship with Patrick was a testament to the healing power of love and trust. Her optimism about motherhood reflected her resilience and determination to shape her own destiny, despite the challenges she faced.

Alice persisted in using her platform to advocate for mental health, sharing her personal experiences to inspire others. She remained a vocal supporter of Women's Aid, using her own past to offer hope and support to those in similar situations. Every post, public appearance, and interview presented an opportunity for Alice to connect with people and make a positive impact.

As Alice looked ahead to the future, she did so with optimism and a sense of purpose. She had not only achieved success in her life, but also found meaning by using her influence to uplift others. Her journey served as a powerful reminder that it is possible to overcome even the most difficult pasts and emerge stronger, more compassionate, and ready to face any challenges that may come.

With the love of her family, the support of her partner, and her own unwavering determination, Alice Liveing had discovered a way to transform her pain into strength. Her story was far from finished, and as she continued to write each new chapter, she knew she was not alone and that her journey could inspire others.

Chapter Eight
Give Me Strength

Alice Liveing was filled with anticipation as she stood in the midst of a busy bookstore in London. The launch event for her new book, *Give Me Strength: How I Turned My Back on Restriction, Nurtured the Body I Love, and How You Can Too,* was just about to commence. It was July 4th, and the room was buzzing with a mixture of friends, family, fans, and members of the press. The journey that had led Alice to this moment had been challenging, and she couldn't help but reflect on the difficult path she had taken.

Back in 2017, Alice had reached the pinnacle of her career. Known as Clean Eating Alice, she was the most prominent personal trainer in the UK. With a staggering half a million followers on Instagram, she had become a household name. Celebrities sought her advice, she graced the cover of

Women's Health magazine, and she had achieved three best-selling books according to the Sunday Times. From the outside, she appeared to be the epitome of health and success. However, behind the carefully curated social media posts and her radiant smile, Alice was struggling.

Her relationship with food had become disordered, and she was addicted to exercise. What had initially started as a journey towards better health had transformed into an unhealthy obsession with being thin and striving for perfection. Her every waking moment was consumed by restrictive eating habits and exhausting workout routines. The admiration she received online only fueled her compulsion to maintain an unattainable level of fitness.

Alice reached her breaking point when she was given an ultimatum by her concerned friends and family. They were worried about her declining health and mental state, so they staged an intervention and gave her a clear choice: continue on her destructive path or take control of her life and well-being. This moment forced Alice to confront her deepest fears and insecurities.

With the support of her loved ones, Alice began the difficult process of healing. She sought therapy to address the underlying causes of her disordered eating and exercise addiction. Gradually, she started to unravel the complex thoughts and behaviors that had kept her trapped. Although it was a painful journey, it ultimately led her to a place of true health and happiness.

Alice's recovery wasn't just about regaining her physical health; it was also about finding acceptance and peace with her body and redefining her relationship with fitness. This transformation inspired her to write a book called "Give Me Strength," where she shared her story and the valuable lessons she had learned. Her goal was to connect with every woman who had ever felt inadequate or struggled to love their own body.

The book consisted of both personal reflections and a declaration of beliefs. Alice shared her most vulnerable moments and explained how she overcame them. She introduced four principles of fitness: understanding one's motivations, choosing activities that bring joy, establishing a sustainable routine, and being mindful of the journey. These principles aimed to prioritize one's well-being over appearance.

"Give Me Strength" served as a powerful call to action for women everywhere. Alice challenged the prevailing culture of perfection and restriction, advocating for a more compassionate and comprehensive approach to health and fitness. She emphasized the importance of understanding one's motivations, selecting activities that bring happiness, establishing a sustainable routine, and being mindful of the process.

As Alice stood in the bookstore, she felt a mix of excitement and nervousness. This book was her most personal endeavor yet, and she hoped it would deeply resonate with those who needed it the most. The crowd fell silent as she approached the microphone, prepared to share a piece of her soul with the world.

Alice expressed her gratitude to everyone present, acknowledging that writing her book, *Give Me Strength*, was both challenging and fulfilling. She dedicated the book to those who believed that being thinner would bring them happiness and to those who have faced difficulties in accepting and loving their bodies. Alice shared that she had personally experienced these struggles and assured the audience that there is an alternative path towards nurturing self-love and finding genuine happiness and peace. She hoped that her story and the insights shared in her book would assist others on their own journeys. The room erupted in applause, and Alice felt a sense of relief and gratitude. This moment marked the culmination of years of pain, growth, and transformation, highlighting her resilience and the support she received. Throughout the event, Alice signed books and engaged in conversations with attendees, who shared their own stories of overcoming challenges. Witnessing the sense of community and solidarity, Alice recognized that *Give Me Strength* was more than just a book; it served as a lifeline for those who needed reassurance that they were not alone.

In the months that came after, *Give Me Strength* became a symbol of hope for numerous readers. Alice received letters and messages from women all over the globe, expressing gratitude for her honesty and motivation. Her own journey had reached a complete cycle, and she was now utilizing her influence to inspire and support others in their quest for well-being and contentment.

Despite facing various challenges, Alice Liveing had emerged even stronger and more resolute than before. Her narrative served as a compelling reminder that genuine strength originates from within oneself, and that the most significant transformation occurs in the depths of one's heart.

Printed in Great Britain
by Amazon